How to be a Successful Bastard

A pocket guide for people who are too nice to be successful

Adrian Maile

First published 2009 by SB Publishing

SB Publishing,
PO Box 61628,
London SE12 0XS

Copyright © Adrian Maile 2009

A catalogue record for this book is available from the British Library.

ISBN 9780955771613

10 9 8 7 6 5 4 3 2 1

Printed in China

This book may be ordered from
www.successful-bastards.com
or your local bookshop.

CONTENT$

Foreword

'The person who has no enemies, has no followers.' **Don Piatt**

I am very lazy and greedy and proud of it. If Andrew Carnegie, once the richest man in the world, managed to get fabulously wealthy working just three hours a day, six months of the year and travelling the world socialising, self-indulging and scribbling how-to-get-rich books the other six, so can I. There may well be workers' blood on my hands, like there was on his, but I will wash them before I leave the office.

As you can probably guess I like giving direct orders. It works. I can be rude, argumentative and aggressive and I fear nothing. My bark is as bad as my bite. I am also pretty damn ruthless and unforgiving. I operate like that famously once successful, now dead, bastard Lord Robert Maxwell. Like him, when I walk into a room, people mutter 'The ego has landed.' Short barked orders and telephones hung up before calls have finished work for me as they did for him. One major difference between us is that I will not fail and have to mysteriously drown myself so the wife gets the insurance money, the kids take the blame and I get to be buried in Holy Land after a full-blown state-funeral. I will not fail.

This book will change your mind about what you need to do to be successful. You thought it was hard work, intelligence and luck that made people successful. It is not. You have to be a bastard to be successful. You must be selfish, tough, ruthless and unpredictable – and I will show you how.

At first glance you might think the habits and techniques in this book are deplorable, painful to do and will result in people hating you. On the contrary, they will make you happier, wealthier and more successful and help you to build a wonderful circle of like-minded people around you.

You have no one but yourself to blame if you do not get what you deserve from life. Be like me and squeeze every last drop of pleasure from yours.

Take care,

Adrian

What is a successful bastard?

'The object of war is not to die for your country, but to make the other bastard die for his.' **General George Patten**

In Britain and the United States a 'bastard' means someone whose is dislikeable, someone to be treated with contempt. In Australia, the word 'bastard' is a term of endearment – 'You bastard' means, 'Well done.'

In this book, I use the words 'successful bastard' to mean something in between. Someone you have a sneaking admiration for, someone whose success you envy, but someone who is a bastard all the same. Most successful people have no qualms about being a bastard and are more successful because of that. There is a little bit of the bastard in all of us, but most people are afraid to be a bastard when they need to be.

Successful bastards are the 'lucky' few who have mastered being a total bastard at the exact moments when it will improve their position, but who operate with grace, good humour and intellect despite this. They manage to remain curiously likeable and interesting, developing great loyalty in their chosen circle, despite their dislikeable behaviour. Successful bastards:

- ✓ **Are independently wealthy.**

- ✓ **Get what they want.**

- ✓ **Do what they want.**

All successful bastards display all three of these characteristics and focus on developing them in that order. You need money to get what you want and to be able to do what you want.

The three characteristics tie directly to wealth, power and happiness and you probably think that happiness is the most important. However, would you like to be happy and rich or happy and poor? Come to think of it, I would prefer to be *miserable* and rich than *miserable* <u>and</u> poor. Nothing makes being poor easy.

When you are wealthy, many aspects of your happiness can be enhanced, from the provision of your basic needs through to enhancing your life by having thrilling new experiences. When you are poor, you struggle even to fulfil your basic needs, let alone have anything new to bring sparkle to your existence.

If someone tells you money cannot buy you love, just look at the next rich person's partner you see and ask yourself whether they would be with them if they were a poor, abject failure. Wealth gives no guarantee of happiness, but it certainly helps.

Similarly, if someone tells you that money cannot buy you health, that is true, but it can certainly help a lot. When you have the options of a personal trainer, ten holidays a year, a low stress lifestyle, regular private health screenings, daily massages and the very best nutrition that money can buy, it helps. Add copious leisure time to keep yourself fit the honest way, and you are improving your chances. In the future, good health will be the preserve of the wealthy and the lucky few. Do not take the risk of hoping you will be lucky with your health.

Wealth is the key to starting the cycle.

Power and happiness are the wonderful
by-products:

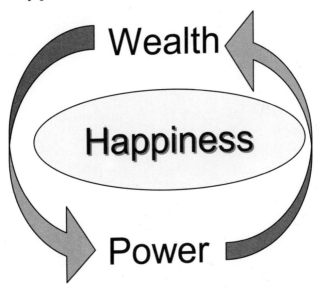

So how do some people make so much
money, so much more than others? All
wealthy people became that way because

they are one of the following types. They are either uniquely talented, lucky or self-made.

If they are uniquely talented, physically or intellectually, then they get paid a lot for doing something that comes naturally. They might be the professional sportsman, the gifted singing prodigy, the stunning catwalk model or a financial whiz. People pay them fortunes for what they have to give using only their natural resources and time. Often what they do comes easy to them. You might say they have raw, unique talent.

Other people are lucky. They get their wealth because someone gave it to them – they inherited it when someone died, they won it or they found it. A British newspaper, *The Sunday Times,* publishes a Rich List annually and it is interesting to note that in 1989, when the first Rich List was launched, 75 per cent of the people in it had inherited their wealth, but in 2007 the fortunes of 78 per cent of the people in it was self-made.

Even if you inherit a fortune, your success is not guaranteed. Look at the unfortunate Jamie Blandford, heir to the fabulous wealth of the dukedom of Marlborough, whose love affair with pharmaceuticals and alcohol led his father to disown him, caused him to spend a month in prison for forging prescriptions, a further 6 months in the slammer and suffer a 3½-year driving ban for dangerous driving and criminal damage following a road-rage incident. You still need to be smart to get that inheritance and then subsequently hang onto it.

The odds are against you having a unique talent or being lucky, so you are unlikely to make money this way. Which leaves you only one sure way to get rich – you have just got to be self-made.

This book explains how you can become a self-made success. It is crammed with useful techniques and examples and is organised in such a way that you can either read it front-to-back or just dip in and out as you see fit. The book will show you how to exploit your limited potential, talents and resources to be successful. It is titled *How to be a Successful Bastard* because it gives you that extra chance over the competition by telling you the secrets that successful bastards use to get wealthy, powerful and happy:

✓ **All successful, self-made, uniquely gifted or just plain lucky people are one sort of bastard or another at some time in their lives.**

✓ **To make it, hold onto it and enjoy it, successful people have to be self-centred, tough, ruthless and unpredictable.**

✓ **Successful people do not share how they operate with ordinary people, so what they know is usually kept secret... until now.**

I will explain the four secret habits of successful bastards. For each habit, I will discuss five traits that collectively make the habit real. Each trait has five supporting techniques that allow you to develop them fully. So for each habit, you will have 25 techniques to note, observe in others and practise yourself.

When you read any self-help book titled *How to Become a Billionaire* or whatever, there is one fundamental problem with what you read. The author is unlikely to tell you just how much of a bastard the people referenced had to be to succeed in the first place and then to stay there afterwards.

This book is different. It acknowledges that some of the most distasteful behaviours are pre-requisites for a successful lifestyle. You may disagree now, but you will change your mind soon. That said, you will need to behave in ways that today might seem alien to you. You want success and I will show you how.

My only words of caution are: Be careful what you wish for.

Play a game on my website www.successful-bastards.com to hone your skills at spotting how successful bastards' behaviour works.

Lucky bastards

'I believe in luck; how else can you explain the success of those you dislike?'
Jean Cocteau

There is no such thing as luck, just certain behaviours that expose a person to opportunity. If you want more luck, open your eyes and be more of a bastard.

Since there is no such thing as luck, there is no such thing as a lucky bastard. However, there are bastards for sure. We just assume that all the successful ones must be lucky. They are not. They work hard at being bastards and what looks like luck follows them around.

If you do not believe me, just read Richard Wiseman's book, *The Luck Factor*. Richard is a psychologist and has been researching what makes people lucky for fifteen years. His conclusion is that people we might call 'lucky bastards' make luck happen through their attitude and behaviour. Attitudes and behaviours you will discover in the habits, traits, tips and techniques within this book.

Once you can spot the opportunity to make your own luck, you will have to be committed to making that thing happen positively in your favour, at all costs. Other bastards will be looking to exploit the same opportunity, and it is the biggest bastard that will keep hold of it and benefit from it.

The quick bastard test
Name three rich, successful people you know personally and work out from what you know of them how much of a bastard they are. Which of the following character traits get ticked as applying to them?

	Person #1	**Person #2**	**Person #3**
They love themselves			
They are tough to deal with			
They never give up			
You cannot second guess them			
Total score			

(If you do not know three rich, successful people, you need this book more than you thought. Skip the next bit and just get on with reading the book and practising being a bastard more often.)

I bet all three of the people you selected score at least three ticks out of a possible four. Consider what this means. The first three successful people you could think of are bastards. Here is a shocking bit of news for you: all successful people are bastards. Very successful people are egotistical, tough, tenacious and unpredictable bastards.

You cannot be rich, powerful and successful if you are nice, kind, friendly, thoughtful and predictable. It just will not happen. There are too many sharks out there and they will eat you alive if you show signs of weakness.

Many of the most famous captains of industry who are revered as role models for business leaders were evil, manipulative bastards, and I will tell you who they are and what they did. Who would have thought, for instance, that the Astor family, once the richest in the world, would have part-founded their wealth on the back of smuggling narcotics around the world?

To make money, you must exploit others and be prepared to operate in the shadowy world of deceit and corruption that is business.

You might now be saying, 'OK, maybe you do have to be a bastard to be successful, but that is a price I am not willing to pay.' Or, 'I am too nice to be a bastard.'

Wake up, friend. Life is a competitive challenge, not a leisurely break. You get what you deserve. If you want to help others, make a load of money now. You can be as nice as you like when you are older and independently secure.

Successful bastards have everything you want. They have the cars, the houses, the gorgeous spouse, the sex, the friends, the material goods, all the money and all the fun. They represent everything you could have been if only you had had a bit more luck. At least that is what you think.

It is OK to be a bastard and be successful. In fact it is the only way to get there if you are an average person. 'Successful bastard' means something different than just a bastard. The word 'bastard' transforms into a good word when used with the word 'successful.' It no longer means someone to be treated with contempt. It means someone you, and others, aspire to become.

✓ **All successful people are one sort of bastard or another.**

- ✓ If you want more luck, be more of a bastard more often.

- ✓ The biggest bastard will keep hold of the biggest opportunity.

- ✓ Wealth is always created by the exploitation of others.

- ✓ Make a load of money now and you can be as nice as you like when you are older and financially independent.

First steps to success

The first step in basic training is to make a decision to change how you judge things around you. You have to learn to see the world differently. Think of life as a gloriously complex and advanced game; play to win, play hard, take no prisoners and have fun. You are a player and almost everybody else on the planet is playing against you. Life is

supposed to be highly competitive. Ask
Charles Darwin.

Your competition will fall into one of five
groups of people:

Wimps	lightweight, boring, failures
Whingers	miserable, depressed saboteurs
Wasters	Time-wasting, high-maintenance nuisances
Wankers	jumped-up, pompous idiots
Winners	self-centred, tough, ruthless risk takers

The first four groups are the targets of your
contempt. Think of them as your enemies. At

best they will slow you down; at worst they will actively compete against you. Be a bastard to all of them. They will do nothing for you, so be brutal.

Only the *winners* get your respect. They are the people with whom you will operate as near equals, with whom you will plan and build your success. If you are fortunate, your close associates are already all winners. If not, you'd better get to work on the ones that are not immediately.

There will not be many winners, so choose them carefully. Know who they are soon. Some will be found in your immediate family, close friends or trusted lieutenants, but most are out there for you to find in new acquaintances.

THE FOUR SECRET HABITS OF SUCCESSFUL BASTARDS

Look after number one

Wield your power

Never give up

Keep everyone guessing

HABIT No. 1: Look after number one

'To love oneself is the beginning of a lifelong romance.' **Oscar Wilde**

Life is not a team sport. You play alone. You come into the world with nothing and leave the same way, so do not waste any time while you are here. Above all else, look after number one.

If you are successful so will your family and so will your friends and colleagues. However, if you fail to put yourself first, everyone around you will fall by the wayside.

Nobody ever remembers the name of the silver or bronze medal winner. How many CD music compilations have you seen on sale titled 'Greatest Number 2s of the

1980s'? The gap between first and second can be miniscule, but the difference is gigantic. Play to win every time.

In some cultures, particularly in Britain, people have a peculiar distaste for winners. This stems from the basic beliefs of 'justice' and 'fair play' that pervade the culture. The successful bastards among us know that this culture creates losers, not winners.

I am sure in your life there have been times when you have focused on what you want to do. You have been indulgent and spoiled yourself. Have a think about some of those times now…

If, like most people, you rarely indulge yourself, you will have struggled to remember the last time you did exactly what you wanted to do, but you will I am sure have remembered one or two occasions when you did. They were good weren't they? You felt good afterwards.

Successful bastards indulge themselves all the time. They feel good about themselves all the time. They put themselves first.

Most people go through life thinking about other people and how their own actions impact on those around them. On the other hand, successful bastards never think about other people unless they can further their own interests by doing so. They think the world revolves around them. They take self-satisfaction to its limit.

The *Queen of Mean*, Anne Robinson – journalist and broadcaster and now world famous host of *The Weakest Link* TV quiz – describes the culture that her businesswoman mother bestowed upon on her from an early age as being 'last in the queue, first on the bus.' Anne says that she had one ambition in life, 'to be famous' and her self-centred attitude has delivered her just that.

You will discover that when you become more self-centred people will look up to you and admire you even though deep down most would say that being so would make a person dislikeable. When someone describes a self-centred successful person they will use positive adjectives like: 'a real character, clever, charismatic, fun to be with, super-confident, a born winner...' People will always highlight your positive characteristics and overlook the negative ones, so be confident and make sure your nest is fully feathered as quickly as possible.

If you have unfulfilled dreams – think of yourself more often. No one will mind if you do. On the contrary, they fully expect you to.

That is an accepted part of being successful.

Five ways to build your strength
Love yourself, for there is nothing finer in
life. If you do not love yourself, how can you
expect anyone else to love you? You have
potential beyond your wildest dreams so live
up to that potential. Whilst you are at it –
love your money, love material things, love
being a consumer and love your leisure time.
Love things that make the one you love the
most feel good.

Looking after number one is all about you. It
is about being focused on what you want,
focused on you – being self-centred. There is
nothing wrong with being self-centred. On
the contrary, it is a pre-requisite for success.
When the going gets tough, being self-
centred will keep you on track.

Strong people are self-centred. Self-centred

people are **confident, competitive, selfish, greedy** and **lazy**. By developing these traits you will have five ways to be more self-centred.

✓ **Believe in yourself.**

✓ **Play to win, no one remembers who came second.**

✓ **Put yourself first.**

✓ **Indulge and spoil yourself.**

✓ **Fulfil all your dreams.**

HABIT No. 2:
Wield your power

'It is better to be feared than loved, if you cannot be both.' **Niccolo Machiavelli**

The game of life is highly demanding, aggressive and potentially dangerous. Other people will be trying to win and they will be competing against you. If you assume that they will stop at nothing to win, you had better retaliate before they attack. Assume that people will try and get one over on you at the first opportunity, so be prepared to use the pre-emptive strike by demanding the best and being tough enough to stay the course.

If you are cunning, your premature retaliatory gestures will keep people in check and make sure that they do not begin to consider attacking you. Subconsciously they will think that if you are like this when they are not attacking you, god only knows how troublesome you will be if they do. They will not be able to pluck up the courage to initiate anything against your wishes.

Attack is the best form of defence in many situations. As they say, every battle is won before it starts. Read Sun Tzu's *The Art of War*, to develop your strategies fully.

Getting your retaliation in first advances the battle faster than your opponents can keep up with. It creates engagement when others are not ready to compete, thereby weakening their position dramatically. It creates a platform for success moulded to what you want to happen, not what someone else does. It makes you appear a formidable opponent from the outset.

Five ways to be formidable
Powerful people use force and in doing so they are tough to deal with. Tough people are demanding, rude, argumentative, critical and aggressive. By developing these traits you will have five ways to make yourself tougher. Being tough means you can influence others easily and make sure you neutralise opposition before it gathers momentum.

- ✓ **Attack is often the best form of defence.**

- ✓ **Retaliate before anyone attacks.**

- ✓ **Master the pre-emptive strike.**

- ✓ **Justice and fair play creates losers, not winners.**

- ✓ **Be formidable.**

HABIT No. 3:
Never give up

'We are not retreating – we are advancing in another direction.
General Douglas Macarthur

Failure is not an option once you are committed to playing the game. You must be ruthlessly unstoppable. Your aims and objectives must be met – every time. If you get everything done your way you will open up the beautiful world of satisfaction that successful bastards enjoy.

Shake off the fear culture of losers. Make yourself a winner by making definite decisions and keeping focused on achieving your aims. Never give up. Get what you want done and get it done your way.

Duncan Bannatyne, the famous British entrepreneur, went from being a Navy stoker to building a £115 million fortune by doing things his way and never giving up. Bannatyne believes '....you never need to pay for an expensive consultant.' In all his businesses – from old peoples' homes and hotels to fitness clubs and casinos – Bannatyne got things done his way by investing his own money and making key decisions based on common sense.

Bannatyne might believe his success in building his businesses rests on his skilful delegation to his management team, but it is clear that his original businesses were first established because he was fearless and ruthless in pursuing his aims. He did whatever it took to be successful.

You too must be prepared to fight relentlessly and determinedly for what you want. You must also be prepared to punish anyone who stands in your way. You will have to be cruel to be kind to anyone who presents barriers to your success.

Five ways to be unstoppable
People who never give up are ruthless. Ruthless people are fearless, incisive, determined, unforgiving and cruel. These traits collectively provide an important weapon in the successful bastard's arsenal.

Deep down everybody feels frightened at times. Adrenalin is a gutsy hormone. It makes our bodies react to fearful situations and encourages 'fight or flight' responses in our nervous systems. Use it to your advantage.

- ✓ Shake off the fear culture.

- ✓ Make firm decisions and stick to them.

- ✓ Never surrender.

- ✓ Punish failure.

- ✓ Be cruel to those who stand in your way.

HABIT No. 4: Keep everyone guessing

'The President has kept all of the promises that he intended to keep.' George Stephanopolous (aide to Bill Clinton)

On those rare occasions when someone has got one over on you, I bet you have mostly been surprised and felt let down. I bet you have been surprised that the person or organisation could do it to you and have been left reeling from the experience. If you knew it was coming, it came as less of a shock and when it did, you were able to deal with it more quickly, rationally and completely than if it had been unexpected.

Use the power of the dagger while hiding it under your cloak. Make sure that people cannot read you or predict your next actions. Be prepared to change tack when needed and to let people down on a whim. Think nothing of being duplicitous and dishonest to compete with those around you. Take the sorts of risks that others would not dare to, and live life on the edge.

You may think my prescription would result in an unpleasant life, that it will be distasteful to be unfathomable and unreliable. On the contrary, it makes for a comfortable and predictable existence for you and that is all that matters.

Anything goes as far as you are concerned, and people will get used to your eccentric and confusing behaviour. They know you will stop at nothing to achieve your aims, and whilst everyone around you is trying to second guess what you will do, you will be free to pursue whichever direction takes your fancy, no matter how risky it may appear.

Five ways to be unpredictable
Staying one step ahead requires judicious use of your cloak and dagger. You need to be a person of mystery and intrigue, difficult for others to judge. You need to keep people guessing what your next move will be. You must be unpredictable.

Unpredictable people are **enigmatic, deceptive, unreliable, dishonest and reckless**. Developing these traits will give you that maverick character that will make you difficult to deal with and an impressively mysterious persona that will keep all your enemies panicking about your next move. Reckless disregard for the laws of the land will allow you to exploit every opportunity for making money and hanging onto it.

- ✓ Use your cloak and dagger
- ✓ Confuse people
- ✓ Create mystery
- ✓ Do whatever it takes
- ✓ Be prepared to risk everything

DEVELOPING THE HABIT$ OF $UCCE$$FUL BASTARD$

#1. Look after number one – Being self-centred

Building self-confidence: Techniques to make you more confident

'Confidence is a habit that can be developed by acting as if you already had the confidence you desire to have.'
Brian Tracy

1. Be sure of yourself. Extend your assertiveness into arrogance. The dividing line is so thin that no one will notice. Everyone is good at something, so know what your something is. Even if you think you are unskilled you are not. Maybe you are good at watching TV. So are TV reviewers. Maybe you are good at drinking. So are publicans. Maybe you are good at crosswords, stacking shelves, spotting errors in newspapers or making people laugh. Whatever it is, it is a skill and something that you can exploit to your advantage.

How many times have you known you were right to say or do something, but because you lacked confidence you gave in and did not say what you wanted to? You did not trust your expertise. Always say what you think and do what you feel.

There was a joke circulating in the 1990s about Larry Ellison, founder and CEO of Oracle Corporation. The joke sums up a man being sure of himself most perfectly:

Q: What's the difference between God and Larry Ellison?

A: God doesn't think he's Larry Ellison.

This question amazingly became the title of Larry's *authorised* biography, so there is a clue there somewhere about how far you can take your own self-confidence if you want to be very successful.

For study purposes, watch anyone who has made a ridiculous amount of money in a short space of time or the manager of any top class professional sports team.

2. Be clever. The difference between being clever and intelligent is that clever people know what to do with what intelligent people know. Surround yourself with intelligent people, not clever people. Then you will stand out. If you are not sure about something ask a clever person. You will get the right answer, unless you are competing, in which case they will lie.

Being clever has got nothing to do with IQ. The average IQ is 100. Around 75% of the population is between 90 and 110. I am 140, by the way, but as my father-in-law reminds me, I am just good at doing IQ tests. I am sure his opinion might have something to do with the fact that he finds them difficult, but I tend to agree with him. My brother-in-law, Tony Newton, is a greengrocer turned gardener. He does not have a high IQ, and he left school at 14, but he is the cleverest person I know. He knows the value of everything, has a fantastic eye for a deal, is a superb judge of character and he controls and uses his money more wisely than anyone. He has a roguish manner and always has plenty of money.

There is no need to be well-educated, just to

develop your ability to realise the value of stuff – information, relationships and things. The list of famous and wealthy people who dropped out of college because they had better things to do is very long. Being clever means that you need to know a little of what is worth knowing and nothing of what is not. Do not waste time on all the finer detail of knowledge. Find the lowest common denominator and use your intuition.

Get to know the details. The key word is 'know.' Data is the basis of information, and when information has a use it becomes knowledge. You do not need to know all the data, just the important information. Get to the hub of any issue, find out the data that answers the key questions and use this to improve your position.

Tony Blair, the former Prime Minister of Britain, stayed in power by surrounding himself with people who were experts in extracting key information from data and then delivering it to him as knowledge. He valued such people very highly. In 2004, he even supported a former Cabinet Minister, called Peter Mandelson, who was widely disliked and had been twice disgraced by scandal. Blair brought him back from political exile by offering him the job of European Commissioner when it was Britain's year to head the Commission.

Like Mr Blair, always seek the key information that can be used to make an intellectual point or gain a competitive advantage. Use the knowledge gained as a weapon. Once you know what others do not, you are in a position of considerable power.

3. Stay cool under pressure. Do NOT get stressed about anything. Do not worry or get depressed. Look relaxed and comfortable at all times. It helps if you do not think too hard about what is happening around you. Most people get stressed because they make themselves too busy; they take on too much in too little time. Play things by ear. See how the cookie crumbles. See how the wind blows. 'Shoot the breeze' a little.

I love the story Donald Trump recalls in one of his many books. In the early 1990s he had accumulated insurmountable debt and was facing potential bankruptcy at the hands of his creditors. He passed a vagrant on the pavement one day thought: 'He was worth $9.2 billion more than I was.'

Trump survived the spectre of bankruptcy, restructured his finances and moved on. In 2006, his net worth was estimated to be US$4.2 billion. Today, he is more famous, wealthy and popular than ever, thanks in part to his TV show, *The Apprentice*, which earns him reportedly US$3 million per episode – a nice bit of pocket money for what he describes as his 'hobby.'

If you think your overdraft is a bit high, stay cool and deal with it. For study purposes watch any poker professional who has won a world title or any billionaire.

4. Look smart. If you want to be successful, you must first look successful. Buy fewer, but more expensive, clothes. Wear one or two pieces of jewellery, and buy the best you can afford. Start with a watch; add a ring and that is usually enough. Too much jewellery will make you look ridiculous – a target for muggers – and will distract the people you are trying to influence, so do not fall into that trap.

Be well-groomed and develop the skill of looking smart in casual wear. Most people

look like paupers when they dress down.
This will do you no good. Keep some very
special items for those casual days.

Try to emulate someone like Sven Goran
Eriksson, the multi-millionaire and former
football manager – the only one to have won
the league-and-cup double in three different
countries (Sweden, Portugal and Italy).
Eriksson owns around 150 hand-tailored
suits. 'Sven takes pride in his appearance and
has a collection of very expensive bespoke
suits that he has built up over the years,' a
source told one tabloid.

For study purposes look at any of the lists
of best-dressed people who are published
in magazines or watch any TV or film
awards ceremony.

5. Stay aloof. When you are a successful
bastard, you look down on the masses of

people yet to discover how to become one. You also look down on people who will criticise, complain and try to compete with you. Look down your nose at people. If you find this difficult, get yourself a pair of designer glasses with small lenses and just perch them on the end of your nose.

A slightly more expensive way to remind you to be aloof is to get a luxurious penthouse at the top of a landmark building in a big city.

I hope one day to have something like 'The Donald' has. His home occupies the top three floors of Trump Tower on 5th Avenue in New York City. It helps you to believe in yourself when you have a US$50 million apartment, on the top three floors of a tower named after you, bedecked in gold, bronze and marble, offering 3,000 m² to bounce around and count your money in.

For study purposes watch any small town magistrate, anyone who is senior mason or anyone who is making enormous sums from corrupt business activity. It may save you time if this is all one and the same person.

Before you move onto building your competitive skills, get firmly grounded and really believe in yourself. You are special. Don't get weighed down with complex detail when some key facts are best. Act relaxed at all times and dress smartly as you rise far above everyone around you.

Becoming a key player: Techniques to make you more competitive

'I play to win, whether during practice or a real game.' **Michael Jordan**

6. Be ambitious. Someone who is ambitious has a strong desire for success. For most people, this means getting lots of power and wealth. You would not be reading this book if you did not have at least some desire to be more successful, and you are probably very ambitious.

Some people, usually the failures, dislike ambition and see it is a negative characteristic of people. That is, of course, bullshit spread by successful bastards themselves. They keep the masses under control by stifling individual ambition.

Ambition is what makes dreams a reality. It is the driving force that enables people reach their goals. Ambition is based not on a vague wish, it is a decision. Know what you want and it will make life much easier. If you know what you want and where you want to be, ambition gets you there.

Set clear goals for yourself, make them public and go for it. Your goals must be tangible and time-bound, and above all simple. They should be something like:

- ✓ Big house by 25
- ✓ New Ferrari by 30
- ✓ Two-kid family by 35
- ✓ Retirement by 40

Do not worry about being overly ambitious. If you are, you will get farther than by being moderately ambitious. Tell your boss that you want his/her job and ask them when you can have it. If they do not tell you, ask your boss's boss.

Better still, resign, take what you know with you and create your own business doing the same thing, but better. It is the only way to make real money.

For study purposes watch the eldest child of any successful entrepreneur after they are appointed CEO of the family corporation whilst still in their early twenties.

7. Seize opportunity. Look at everything in terms of the opportunity presented to you. Opportunities can be classified into three types. Every opportunity will relate to money, exposure or enjoyment – ideally all three. Assess every situation in terms of these and quickly assess the return you will get for the effort you put in. If it does not feel worthwhile instantly, do not pursue it.

Sir Richard Branson, one of our best-loved entrepreneurs and businessmen, seizes the opportunity like no one else– especially if it includes some gratuitous self-promotion. When British Airways decided to stop flying Concorde, Branson was immediately on the Government's case, offering to pay £1 each for the supersonic birds that remained in service, highlighting that this was what British Airways had effectively paid the UK Government when the company was privatised. He even had Concorde models constructed with the Virgin Atlantic logo positioned prominently on them on display on his desk when interviewed at the time for television news.

Whether Branson truly intended to take on the loss-making and hugely expensive fleet of ageing aircraft is not known, but he did not miss the opportunity to get one over on his major competitor at that time by saying that he did. You too should seize every opportunity, even if you do not really want it – you never know where it might lead.

8. Play to win. Show me a good loser and I will show you someone who does not win very often. The joy in winning is something that winners know well and losers have no clue about. Until you win, you think that it is ok just to have played and you cannot see what all the fuss is about. Once you start winning you will get a life-long taste for it, I promise you. Start today.

The greatest golfer in the world, Tiger Woods, is arguably the most competitive man alive. His mastery of one of the most difficult sports known to man means he personifies competitiveness perfectly: 'I don't look at what the purse is or the prize money. You play. And when you play, you play to win, period... If you win, everything will take care of itself.'

Everything you do is a competition of one sort or another. Your position in life itself is as a competitor in a giant game. Millions of people are playing against you, competing for what you deserve. Be like Tiger, be committed to winning and beating others. Otherwise, what is the point in competing in the first place? Look at being competitive as a healthy and character-building pastime.

Be the highest paid, the fastest promoted, the person with most knowledge and authority, the driver of the best car, the owner of the best house. Above all, compete and be the best.

Do not bother with autopsies should you lose. You will just upset yourself. Pretend it did not happen. Better still, avoid losing altogether by making and changing the rules to suit you.

For study purposes, watch bookmakers at the race-track or anyone who trades high volumes of anything.

9. Change the rules to suit you. The game successful bastards play has one unique characteristic. They make the rules. Here are two golden rules of mine:

   1) Never tell anyone everything.

   2)

As I said, make your own rules. Write yours down as you go – you will find plenty of inspiration within this book.

A good friend of mine, Andy Baulch, a licensed London taxi driver and my personal chauffeur, is the most naturally competitive individual I know. Andy is a joy to behold in competition. He has developed a sixth sense for extending competitions and changing the rules when he realises that things might not go his way. From the simple 'best of three' darts match that somehow transforms into the 'best of 21' as his opponent outplays him early on, through to the creation of competitions within the competition to make sure he can win.

If Andy is betting on the outcome of a round of golf, for example, he will add new sub-wagers on the outcome of specific shots and holes as soon as he sees the chances of winning the whole match fade. Whatever happens, he finishes victorious somehow.

For study purposes, watch licensed London taxi drivers on the golf course.

10. Change the game to suit you. If you really want to be mega-successful, change the game itself. Swap to another way of making money, make major changes to the current one, or invent a completely new one.

Most of my experience in business has been in the field of technology and that industry is a game changer extraordinaire. Ten years ago, who would have thought that any company could put a camera in a phone and everyone who has one to take videos and load them onto their own website? Now this is one of the most profitable and fastest growing business areas in the world.

You can change the game, even if at a smaller level, and it will have great impact. You know you have some special skills. There are some things you really excel at. You will find that these things are also the things you most enjoy doing. That is because you are good at them and you therefore perform well, which makes you feel good about yourself.

What are the three things that you are the best at doing? Numbers, public speaking, telling jokes, reading fast, acting the fool, listening, saving money, dealing with people… They could be anything, but think hard to come up with those that are the undisputed top three.

Now, armed with this insight about yourself, think how you can use these skills more in your day-to-day money-making efforts. Get more involved in those parts of your life where your skills have the most positive impact on you. Change your job role to be more suited to your skills. Change your profession if necessary.

The people who make fortunes change the way something is made or experienced. They change the game in their favour and as prime movers in the new environment they have an opportunity to flourish before potential competitors can prepare themselves.

For study purposes, watch anyone who works at a senior level with really advanced technology and gets away with looking like someone living on welfare handouts.

Getting what you want: Techniques to make you more selfish

'Selfishness is not living as one wishes to live; it is asking others to live as one wishes to live.' **Oscar Wilde**

11. Do what you want. Instead of saying 'I have to' do something, try saying 'I choose to' do something. If it feels wrong, you should not be doing it. If it feels right, then carry on.

Most people actually do what they want most of the time, but convince themselves that others are making them do it. How much of what you did today felt like free choice? The 'I choose to' technique will help you spot the things that others are making you do, and you can eliminate them from your schedule. Try saying 'No' to people more often. It works wonders.

12. Be an attention seeker. Get people focused on you and what you say about yourself. The easiest way to do this is to talk about your own life all the time. Regardless of the subject, relate every conversation directly to your experience alone and hold the conversation entirely around your amazing exploits in life.

Save your best efforts for when someone is talking about what they have done and people seem interested. Without hesitation state that you have done the same thing but more of it, better, more often, more recently and more successfully.

For study purposes, watch anyone who seeks out unreasonable self-publicity or someone who has never experienced business failure or personal hardship since making their first million at the age of 19.

13. Take all the credit. This involves doing two things well. Know what is going well and what is going badly. Use a phrase like 'I have never been associated with failure' when briefing workers, partners or management, and they will get the message that you will never admit you are wrong and you will blame everyone but yourself if things fail.

Associate yourself with lots of projects and distance yourself from anything that fails. If something fails, it is not your fault and you cannot be held accountable. When things succeed, make sure you write the press release or internal report. Exaggerate your involvement in the successes and remove any evidence of being involved in failures.

For study purposes, watch any male American executive that has his initials on his shirt and tassels on his shoes, any female

American executive that wears red suits or any entrepreneur who made their money 'managing' risks.

14. Be mean. Always say you give donations to charity anonymously, because you say, you do not want the publicity. That way, no one will know that you have not given anything. When you have made and established your fortune and there is no way you can spend it all, then you can become a philanthropist, but in the meantime:

✓ Do not carry large amounts of money with you.

✓ Do not make large cash withdrawals.

✓ Avoid credit cards. Charging their levels of interest should be a crime.

✓ Shop around for everything.

✓ Haggle over the price of everything.

✓ Studiously avoid buying drinks and meals for anyone but yourself.

There are of course exceptions, but these are only reserved for when you are trying to impress others. Lavish parties and expensive entertainment are all very much allowed, but only when the guest list includes people who will subsequently be of use to you.

The most legendary miser yet greatest philanthropist in later life has to be Warren Buffett, the billionaire US investor and head of Berkshire Hathaway, worth an estimated US$52 billion in 2007, is reported to have lent his daughter Susie US$20 to get her car out of the airport garage, but made her write him a cheque there and then to pay him back.

For study purposes, watch anyone who successfully supports a large family and pays the mortgage, whilst earning close to the minimum wage, or any billionaire.

15. Never share anything. Ownership is everything. With ownership comes the authority to make important decisions, craft things your way and above all to get the benefits derived by whatever it is you own. Never ever share your business with anyone. Most partnerships collapse anyway.

For study purposes, look at anyone who has been involved in a failed business partnership or bankrupt family business, or currently owns a business that operates only in a far-off country than the one they reside in.

Getting more of what is good:
Techniques to make you greedier

'Greed is all right; by the way I think greed is healthy. You can be greedy and still feel good about yourself.' **Ivan F Boesky**

16. Get everything you want. So many people feel guilty about satisfying their desire for material things. There is no point in having wealth if you do not spoil yourself with it. If you want something, get it. You deserve it.

My friends often comment on my shoe collection, watches and hand-made suits, art collections, my cars and my houses. They always do this in a positive, albeit slightly amazed, kind of way. They never think I am being stupid or wasting my money. They know it is mine. They just find it amazing that I can have so much beautiful stuff.

One of the best exponents at having everything he wants is Elton John. He has flats, mansions and villas around the world. On one occasion, when he was in court litigating against his accountants for not keeping track of his wealth to his satisfaction, it came to light that he had spent £293,000 on cut flowers in an 20 month period from January 1996. The opposing barrister, in an attempt to show Elton as a man of ridiculous excess, asked him how he could justify spending this fantastic amount. Elton replied simply, 'I like flowers.'

17. Get the best. Surround yourself with the best and most amazing things. Be a fully committed materialist. It is your wealth for you to enjoy. Only buy the best things. They look better and last longer and have a lower lifetime cost. There is one wonderful aspect of being able to buy nice things. You can enjoy them AND make more money in the process. It is just one superb fringe benefit of a being successful bastard.

Buying really expensive things can become a real money-spinner and even a business in its own right. Art, antiques, property and classic motor cars are just some of the extravagances that will appreciate in value as they get older. Add to that the fact that you are a famous person who once owned them and they will sell at a premium at auction because of it.

When you have beautiful material things, secure them well. Over-insure them, keep the receipts and safely store them away. Keep a detailed asset register so that you can prove what you own. Mark the goods in some way so that you can physically show that they are yours should they go astray.

For study purposes, watch any wealthy

entertainer or self-made businessman with a really nice hairdo.

18. Get more than you need. As an ambitious person, you will naturally develop a healthy dissatisfaction with what you have. You will always want more – always want to go one better.

If you cannot afford more, get someone to lend you the money until you have accumulated your own. Robert Earl, the Hard Rock Café founder, was once asked how it felt to be a multi-millionaire after he sold his restaurant chain to Rank Leisure. His response was, 'I have always lived like a millionaire – the difference now is that I have the money.'

For study purposes, watch royalty or anyone of Middle-Eastern appearance that has five names or more, including two that are hyphenated or anyone with an 'al' in their name that is not a shortening of Alan, Albert, Alexander or Alistair.

19. Think BIG. Why waste something as precious as a conscious thought on insignificant things? Think big.

20. Consume heavily. With all you have, you need to experience the joy of abundance fully. You do not see many wealthy people looking slim and fit. Their size reflects their status. Open up the world of gastronomic extravagance. Fine food and wine are joyful. Abundance is overwhelming. You will soon build a tolerance for banquets and indulgent mega-parties. As your consumption grows, people will respect you further. You are enjoying what you deserve.

For study purposes, watch any head chef, anyone big in the corporate hospitality sector, internationally known opera singers or anyone who knows about antique pottery.

Making better use of your time: Techniques to make you lazier

'I do not want to achieve immortality through my work… I want to achieve it through not dying.'   **Woody Allen**

21. Only do what you must. Write down the three things you MUST do yourself as part of your money-making effort. Be very hard on yourself. They must be things that only YOU can do. Then re-organise your life around these.

I am a writer, so you might think I would have to be brilliant at grammar and punctuation. I am not. Microsoft does the main bit and then I just get my Dad to review the copy and he corrects everything. Many famous authors write terrible prose and it then gets corrected by proof-readers and editors.

The one problem with using agents and publishers is that, like venture capitalists, they expect a high return for using their skills and connections. They are also notoriously careful with what they invest in.

It is of course okay for J K Rowling to demand a large slice of profits because her Harry Potter books, films and merchandise are guaranteed to make money. But most authors get very little for their books when publishing their first work. Even the great Ms Rowling's work was rejected by eight publishers before Bloomsbury made their best decision ever and signed her up.

For study purposes, watch anyone who has been married more than twice or has had a life-threatening experience more than once.

They may of course be the same person.

22. Delegate. You cannot do everything yourself, so do not try. Successful bastards only do what is necessary themselves, and then get others to do the rest. Delegation makes a lot of sense. If you do not delegate then it is only your effort that can generate wealth and that limits your potential. Why keep a dog and bark yourself, as they say.

There are a few choices you can make when presented with something that needs to be done: You can DO it, DELAY it, DELEGATE it or DUMP it. Never delay it, it will not happen. If you cannot do it because it is not one of your short-listed tasks, either dump it or delegate it. I recommend doing both in equal measure.

23. Avoid hard work. Hard work is bad for you. Work smart not hard. Most of what you do now is probably pointless, so do not stay buried in the overwork trap. If something is too tough, you should not be doing it yourself anyway.

Develop the ability to present other people's ideas as your own by getting someone to brief you on important things just before you need to talk about them. That way you will not waste time learning stuff you will never use again.

For study purposes, spend some time with someone who is a sleeping partner in a booming business, has invented a game show or who deals in massive quantities of illegal substances.

24. Work part-time. At one all-day business meeting I attended a guy arrived at 12pm after a heavy session in the hotel bar the night before. Instead of an apology he announced, 'Oh, you were obviously not told that I do not do mornings', in response to what he saw of our surprise at his relaxed demeanour. Brilliant. He totally deflected any criticism and his lateness was ignored by everyone. This is a great technique for allowing you to get away with doing half-days. Just make sure that people know you will not be there and it will be tolerated.

Develop some work-related activity that allows you to go and play golf, go to fine restaurants, go to glorious country houses for seminars and generally go to places where no one will know how many hours you work whilst there. Ideally work and play should become indistinguishable.

For study purposes watch anyone who plays a sport professionally.

25. Take lots of holidays. Everybody loves a holiday. Most people only get one holiday per year, or two if they are lucky. Successful bastards seem to go on holiday all the time. They have a year-round suntan, which clearly has not been the result of a few sessions on a cheap sun-bed. Take holidays frequently. They are good for you.

Successful bastards have holiday homes in places that are sunny all year round. They make sure that they get to visit their villa in Portugal, or wherever, at least once a month and make a point of letting you know this. They are the sort of people who when you phone them on a Thursday, they answer with a jaunty and exaggerated 'Hello', and then proceed to tell you that they are on the beach having a spot of lunch and therefore could they call you back later on.

Even if you are constrained by having only

four or five weeks holiday in your job, you can extend this to 10 weeks or more by taking regular long weekends and claiming the days time off in lieu of some fictitious over-time that you claim to have worked. If you are self-employed, independently wealthy or the boss of your own business then the term 'holiday' should have little relevance to you. Every day should be a holiday, with work being a minor distraction.

For study purposes, watch anyone who works as a porter in a large flower or fruit and vegetable market or someone who has taken early retirement from the police force, ideally through supposed ill-health.

#2. Wield your power – Being tough

Achieving the impossible: Techniques to make you more demanding

'Perfection is our goal, excellence will be tolerated.'   Anon

26. Be impatient. You are not here for long, and your time is precious. Your impatience reflects your desire to get things done your way, fast, so be as impatient as you like, as often as you like. Demand things are done quickly. Forget about perfection, just get the job done and finished as best as possible in the shortest time.

When dealing with a time waster, imagine that you are going through customs, late for a flight and whoever is talking to you is one of those pesky customs officials searching for that miniscule nail file inadvertently left in your wash bag that showed up as a tiny blur on their X-ray machine.

Clear up disagreements quickly so that you can snuff them out before they gather steam.

27. Expect the unachievable. Teamwork is when a lot of people do what you say. Make your orders clear and unambiguous – what, when, where and how are important. Why is unimportant. (If asked, explain that it is because you said so.)

When you expect the unachievable, you get often get it. I once asked a very senior executive at Cisco Systems, Wim Elfrink, how our services business was going to overcome what appeared to be an impossible goal – to increase profitability above the already world-record levels.

His reply was swift and direct, 'At Cisco we achieve the impossible.' That was the end of the discussion and I could not really argue with him, now could I? What could I say that would intelligently challenge such a statement? It was a great lesson in what I call 'Execu-speak.'

If anyone questions your expectations, knock them back like Wim did to me. Put such doubters in their place by reminding them, helpfully, that bumble-bees should not be able to fly, that miracles happen all the time and that we are only constrained by what we believe is possible. If they continue to complain, simply fire them and find another masochist to achieve the impossible and line your pockets in the process.

28. Be unreasonable. Never be pleased with anything. Whatever it is, or has been done to you, complain vigorously about it whenever you can. Reject ideas with clenched fists. Get mad about everything. Never miss an opportunity to complain about your job, salary, your car, your house, your last holiday, the meal you are eating, the wine...

If you get bored complaining about things that are under your control, start complaining about things you have little or no influence over, like the weather, the delayed train, your company or your boss, global warming... Anyone and anything are your legitimate targets.

Elton John famously complained to hotel staff when staying at a top London hotel that the wind outside was too noisy. Quite what he was expecting to be done about it, God only knows.

29. Be bossy. When you are being bossy, raise the volume and slow the speed of your speech so that it sounds like every word has an important meaning. People will hang on your every word. People will really listen hard and even if you are talking bollocks, it will sound intelligent and interesting. Force people to listen to you. You are called 'the boss' for good reason.

Ignore the crap about leadership, empowerment and team working. This has been written either by people who refuse to admit that they were successful because they were tough bastards, or by people who have interviewed them and been hoodwinked.

Your life is too short to be run by a committee. You decide what needs to happen, then get people to do it. Bossy is a word used to describe someone telling people what to do. How can anyone be successful if people do not do what the boss wants them to do? No one really likes being told what to do, so some bosses make it look like they have allowed sub-ordinates to make decisions themselves. I advise you to bypass the pretence. Tell them what you want and when you want it done by. It is quicker and easier and you will get what you want done.

30. Be inflexible. Do not allow yourself to be manipulated. Manipulate others instead. Negotiate with people, for sure, but know your minimum acceptable position as well as your best possible. Never allow any movement below your minimum acceptable one. I use the phrase 'that's not acceptable' a lot. No need to say any more than that. Being inflexible does not mean telling people what is acceptable. That is for you to know and them to find out. Learn to be inflexible. It works in your favour.

For study purposes, watch the senior salesperson at a car dealership that has more than 100 sparklingly clean second-hand cars on the forecourt.

Keeping others in their place: Techniques to make you ruder

'People who are smart get into MENSA. People who are really smart look around and leave.' **James Randi**

31. Be abrupt. Use short, punchy, authoritative sentences. Ideally interrupt people when doing so. Raise your voice enough so that people know you are serious. You can interrupt by looking at your watch whilst someone is talking to you. If they fail to spot you doing it and rush to a close, try tapping it as if to check it is still working. This is sure to make them stop talking quickly. State your point and move on.

Send very short, de-personalised e-mails. Capital letters in a bold typeface are great for getting the point across that you are, in essence, raising your voice. If communicating by phone, use 'telephone terrorism.' Hang up when you have stated what you want done and always make sure you end the conversation.

For study purposes, watch anyone senior in the newspaper business; TV personalities who specialise in politics, the media or the arts; or anyone from Eastern Europe.

32. Be ignorant. When you are wealthy and powerful, you will become a celebrity. People like celebrities. They will want to be around you to share in the experience of your wonderful life. You will get people's attention whether you like it or not. Lots and lots of people will want to take some of your precious time and energy, so you have no choice but to ignore lots and lots of people. You will not have the time to please everyone and now that you know this, make your life easier immediately by ignoring people from the outset. You will have to do it eventually, so start now. This is the pinnacle of ignorance.

Ignoring people is an art form worth becoming good at. The simplest form of ignoring people is to say nothing and maintain a lengthy silence after the person has finished talking. Hold an inquisitive, but otherwise blank, facial expression and wait for the reaction. Silence is a terrific weapon. Salespeople have used this technique since commerce began.

Ignoring the first objection is the first golden rule of sales. If someone objects to something, simply shut up and look at them. It creates a weird reaction in most people.

Their first thought is 'My objection is so stupid that this guy is doing me a favour by ignoring it.' Their next thought is that maybe they did not hear the objection, so perhaps they should repeat it. However, they are unable to make themselves repeat it, because of the fear that you did hear it and are ignoring it for their benefit, because it is just too stupid an objection for you to respond to.

Silence is golden. Try it when negotiating for anything, anywhere. The longer you hold your tongue, the more things go in your favour. It is amazing.

A useful technique if you find prolonged silence difficult is letting the person finish and then look puzzled and say, 'Sorry?' This usually causes the person to either repeat themselves or tell you that it wasn't really important. Either reaction will suffice initially. One further repetition of the above is usually enough to close down the subject under discussion in your favour.

Taking things a stage further, try repeating what the person has said, as if to show you have listened carefully, but get the details terribly wrong. This usually frustrates the person adequately to end the conversation after a short series of rescue attempts.

Never look into another person's eyes. It shows that you are engaging if you do and gives others an opportunity to assess where you are coming from. The eyes are, as we know, a window to the soul, and a handy tip is to imagine that you would not want anyone looking at yours, so do not let them. Focus on something on the person's face, like a mole, scar or hair, or something that is behind them. Remember you can always look at your shoes if this gets exhausting. You will be branded as a tough-nut within a few seconds of dismissing eye-contact completely. It is a real winner in making opponents feel uncomfortable.

For study purposes, watch any Scandinavian entrepreneur, any successful venture capitalist or anyone who has made so much money that they have lost interest in everything but tracking their wealth through the performance of the stock markets.

33. Be patronising. When you patronise someone you appear to be treating them kindly but hint that they are inferior to you. After all since you know best, and you are the greatest, this should be second nature to you. If you are in any doubt about how to patronise people, just imagine that they are a teenager and you are a dominant parent. Useful phrases are:

'If I were you…'

'In my experience…'

'With the greatest respect…'

'I am sure you realised your mistake and do not need me to point it out, but I would just like to say…'

For study purposes watch anyone in their twenties who has just got an MBA or Doctorate talking to their older boss.

34. Put people down. Finish people's sentences. It annoys them and gives you good practice at guessing what people are going to say. If you are going to keep people in their place properly, ritually humiliate them in front of other people by openly criticising them for the first thing that comes into your head.

For study purposes, watch any senior manager who has made millions from share options by being in the right place at the right time, who never went to university, who reads *The Sun* newspaper and thinks drinking too much is an honourable pastime.

35. Never be polite. There is a big danger with showing people appreciation. People will think you are easily pleased and a bit of a pushover if you show them appreciation or gratitude, so resist the temptation. Keep people on their toes waiting for appreciation and then present them something that is close to it, but is not quite there. 'Thanks' is usually more than enough.

If you spend your life congratulating others and saying how much you appreciate all they have done for you, eventually they will see through this tactic and it will no longer have a positive impact on them, so do not bother. To make this easier, get people around you who are self-motivated, thick-skinned and loyal. Ditch people who need reassurance and support.

For study purposes, watch anyone who has worked for more than 10 years in a financial services trading environment since they left school without any qualifications or anyone who captains an unsuccessful sports team.

Confronting dissent: Techniques to make you more argumentative

'You do not have to agree with me, but it is quicker.' **Anon**

36. Be abrasive. Ruffle the feathers of those around you. It helps to keep people operating at their best if you wear them down continuously. Just like when a person is hungry, they are more alert; if you oppose them gently at all times, they will be more eager to please you.

Being caustic, curt and dismissive will add just the right amount of abrasion to your relationships with others and keep them aware of their most important priority, keeping you happy.

I enjoy watching Michael Winner, the once film director famous for the 'Death Wish' films and now general raconteur and restaurant critic. Winner is the personification of abrasiveness. One actor who worked with him on *Death Wish 3* is quoted as saying: 'The atmosphere on set was drenched in fear. [He] spent most of his time shouting at everyone, except Charles Bronson, of course. But Mr Winner was also very witty and funny, in a vicious way.'

For me, Winner entered my Successful Bastards Hall of Fame when, in 2006, he was offered an OBE in the Queen's 80th Birthday Honours List for his part in campaigning for the Police Memorial Trust. He declined the honour, reminding Her Majesty hilariously that: 'An OBE is what you get if you clean the toilets well at King's Cross Station.'

For study purposes speak to anyone who regularly uses a middle initial in their name, anyone with a badge that says 'Customer Services Representative,' anyone who works in IT Support and of course moody elderly film directors.

37. Be confrontational. If you want to be confrontational, quickly establish an opposing principle. Disagree on principle and do so publicly. My favourite is to say 'that is bollocks' after someone has spoken.

Lord Denis Healey, the ex-Chancellor of the Exchequer, with whom I had the pleasure of dining with one evening, told me that he had a rubber stamp made with the word

'Bollocks' on it that he used to stamp official reports and documents that he thought were nonsense. If it is OK for the Chancellor of the Exchequer to do this, a man who was leading the economy of the nation, it is ok for you and me, too. Get your own stamp made up immediately.

For study purposes watch anyone who is over thirty years old and is still a socialist, anyone who has been dumped by more than three lovers, anyone who files their personal papers meticulously or anyone who really cares what job title is written on their business card.

38. Turn every discussion into an argument. Arguments are competitive discussions. Knowing what you know now about the importance of competitiveness, it is obvious that we should turn every discussion into a battle to be won. Follow the example of my brother Jon and start every discussion with a grimace so as to signal that before long this next chat will develop into a full blown argument.

For study purposes, watch any woman who is over 45 years old and has four or more young children, middle-aged socialists with a big mortgage or anyone who is ugly but has a wonderful body.

39. Make mountains out of molehills.
It may not be important to them, but it is to you. Just because they think that the matter is trivial should not stop you from turning the situation into a national incident.

For study purposes watch anyone with 'inspector' or 'auditor' in their job title, anyone who has given up a professional career to do full-time charity work or anyone who is unfortunate enough to be bi-polar and forgets to self-medicate.

40. Win every argument. An argument is a verbal competition, so you should always aim to win it. Imagine that you are a successful barrister who cross-examines people for a living. They have some simple tricks for tripping people up. Asking the same question repeatedly but in different ways is their favourite. You simply wait for their answers to contradict one another and then you can undermine the person by highlighting the contradiction. This weakens their position by making them look like they don't know what they are talking about.

For study purposes watch anyone who manages a home talk to the person who earns the money to keep it running. However, if you really want to understand how to win arguments without referencing things that happened 30 years ago, watch politicians at debating time or legal counsel whilst they are in court.

Getting perfection: Techniques to make you more critical

'Honest criticism is hard to take – especially when it comes from a relative, a friend, an acquaintance or a stranger.'
Franklin P Jones

41. Be pedantic. Being a pedant is easy. Just focus on pointless and painful levels of detail and correct everything around you that does not meet your expectations, which will be almost everything. Form a view of the perfect world according to you. Make it as detailed as you can, develop and enhance it every day so that it becomes a real and achievable world to you and then set about driving this benchmark into the world around you.

The real beauty of this approach is that everyone around you will strive to achieve the impossible – the perfection that only you can properly visualise. You will be forgiven for not operating in that way yourself, because people will realise that this is your vision, but that making the vision a reality is their job, not yours.

When you are in a position of power, you will be forgiven for not being a great detail person but recognised as one that drives such attention in those around them. You will be described as a visionary, but not a detail person yourself – and amusingly this will endear you a greater gravitas. People will assume that because you are always grilling them about the detail that you remember it, whereas all you will need to do is grill them skilfully.

42. Criticise immediately. If you fail to

make your criticism immediately, you have lost an important advantage. Whenever people are criticised some time after an event, they fail to remember what it was that they actually did that upset and start to reconstruct the incident to try and rebut the criticism. The classic scenario happens at every six-month performance appraisal that any employee has endured and relates to when they are criticised about something, a long time after the fact. They quite rightly ask, 'Why was I not given the chance to repair this problem at the time. It is unfair to bring it up now, and in such vague terms.'

Never delay making a criticism, because as the person making it, you leave yourself open to the standard rebuttal above. You also risk failing to remember enough of the details to make the criticism convincing and relevant. Time blurs the importance of such things, so get your criticism out at the time, immediately after the event occurs.

You will be pleasantly surprised at how people will react. They will thank you for the criticism rather than resent you. They will appreciate the error of their ways, see it with the same eyes that you have and be delighted that you are coaching them so carefully and personally.

43. Focus on the negative. We are built to notice the negative things, so revel in doing this. I will prove this to you. Ask anyone to answer the following question: 'Is a button a good design?'

The answers will be something like this: 'Yes, but... they come loose and fall off, they break, the hole sometimes gets too big for the button, they can be fiddly, if you lose one it can be difficult to find an exact replacement...' Whoever answers will quickly find all the things wrong with the most successful clothes fastener in all of history. This is because we are pre-tuned to spot the things that are negative about something.

How many times have you heard two people talking about someone else in a positive way only? Rarely, I bet. Forget about being positive. Focus on the negative aspects of a situation, person or object.

I am fascinated at how the talent shows of today have highlighted the power of negativity and brought to their 'nasty' star judges such fame and fortune. Everyone enjoys their caustic and barbed comments, and most people see their nastiness simply as 'honesty.'

Watch Simon Cowell, Piers Morgan or any of the judges on *The X-Factor* or other talent shows, or *Strictly Come Dancing*, and you will see people unafraid of being cruelly negative to the people auditioning before them. The best known and most popular judges are the ones who are most often most negative. Deep down we all wish we could speak our minds when we feel negatively about something and we respect people who do, because they are so rare. Focus on the negative and you will be more successful for it.

44. Ignore input. You know you know what is best. Make sure everyone around you knows that you know that you know what is best. Along the way, many people will question your decisions, your approach, your strategy and your style. If they are not in your trusted inner-circle, simply ignore them. You are the boss after all. Almost every really successful person has no advisers, except for a few people who are just like them, other self-made successful bastards. If the advice of a professional adviser is worth taking, why would they not apply it themselves independently and achieve their own success.

Avoid consultants like the plague. They will cost you money, confuse your people and dilute what you direct others to achieve. Believe in your judgement and ignore everyone around you. You may think that this would make people think you are ignorant and narrow-minded. On the contrary people will see that you are committed and single-minded. Remember, that your success will be envied and applauded with equal measure, so just ignore the input of the envious and bask on the applause.

45. Make your criticism personal. There is nothing as effective as making a criticism personal. The best way to achieve this is to direct it at one person, publicly, in front of a group of their peers.

It is a technique that the most powerful businesspeople around the world use to their advantage.

It need not be even aggressive criticism. Any criticism will do, as long as it is personal. Simply ask lots of direct questions, in rapid succession and wait for the person to be unable to answer one – then simply criticise the person by name, very directly and imply that if they cannot manage to answer such a simple question as this, how can he or she be expected to run their part of the business, this project, that branch, this team, etc… with competence.

You may think that this would make people hate you, but bizarrely, the opposite is true. You will be seen as someone who drives others to perform at their very best. People will love you for your direct approach and your courage when confronting weak and underperforming people.

Building a fear culture: Techniques to make you more aggressive

'When you have them by the balls, their hearts and minds will follow.'
Jerry Martin

46. Be loud. Never be afraid to raise your voice. Boom your instructions and orders. Shouting at people is a remarkably powerful weapon. It is disarming to the people and reduces the chance of that person, or anyone within earshot, ever incurring your displeasure again.

Develop the capability to be loud, without being angry. Control your anger and just raise your voice to a deafening volume. Loudness without the normally associated anger is doubly disarming. Most people receive the message immediately and sub-consciously they will accede to your demands immediately, fearing that the next level of your wrath, being loudness AND anger, is something that must be avoided at all costs. The very best exponents at this technique are theatre directors and Shakespearean actors who have to project their voices to be heard. For study purposes watch the actor Brian Blessed.

47. Be abusive. There is nothing like an expletive or two, aimed at a person directly, to make them upset. Swear frequently and crudely. It adds a dimension of menace to what you say. Some very successful bastards have made a foul mouth part of their trademark and are not thought of any the worse for it.

The most successful British chef in history, Gordon Ramsay, a gutsy 40 year old ex-professional footballer, is the only chef in London honoured with three stars by the Guide Michelin. Ramsay has developed a celebrity greater than any of his competitors, and a wealth to match. He is best known for liberally using the word 'fuck' and its derivatives, more than anyone who has ever been in the public eye. He even had a TV series broadcast called 'The F Word.'

He loves abusing people, including his colleagues and competitors alike. He called his ex-boss Marco-Pierre White, to whom he says he owes 'everything,' a 'fat bastard' at his own wedding. Of Ainsley Harriot, another celebrity chef, he said: 'Ainsley's not a chef, he is a fucking comedian.' He is also happy to criticise nationally loved personalities, such as legendary Australian talkback radio host John Laws: 'That John Laws. What a knob. What a fucking knob.'

48. Be bad-tempered. If you wander around with a smile on your face all the time, you will look oily and complacent. Look miserable, threatening and bad-tempered instead. If you behave in a bad-tempered way, people will avoid you. That is good. It means you will spend less effort on time-wasters with pointless ideas and having to deal with stupid people with stupid problems. Only the really important things will come to your attention.

I used to work for a guy in banking who was well-known for being bad-tempered in the morning and drunk in the afternoon. You had a choice if you wanted to get a decision from him. Face a bollocking in the morning or listen to a load of bollocks when he was drunk in the afternoon. You avoided any contact with him whatsoever and just got on with your job. This left the old successful bastard plenty of time in the mornings to recover from his hangover and freed up his afternoons to get slaughtered all-over again.

For study purposes watch elderly police officers who are still in uniform, middle managers with problems at home, anyone with an alcohol or drug problem or anyone who is suffering from an invisible, but critical, illness.

49. Be physical. Verbal assault is one thing, but nothing beats getting physical with people when it comes to making an impressive impact. It does not have to enter into 'Grievous Bodily Harm' territory. Your physical presence alone can be adequately threatening and you can use the power of a very firm handshake or robust pat on the back to establish your position beautifully. If you struggle to intimidate people by touching them firmly, simply throw things at them or gently cuff them around the head.

If you are all-powerful, everyone else must be weak. Therefore, do not feel embarrassed or awkward about bullying the weak, because it includes everyone on the planet, near enough. Survival of the fittest has been a pretty successful model to date. Speak to anyone who was bullied at school in later life and they will tell you all the positive things they got from the experience. It made them tougher, made them stand-up for themselves and made them into the strong person they are today.

For study purposes watch anyone greet another where either person has played a contact sport, was once in the Armed Forces or has studied martial arts to avoid being bullied but failed to grasp the spiritual side of it. To perfect the art of throwing things at people, watch any woman having a row at home with their partner after he has been caught doing something she objects to.

50. Be explosive. When you get upset, do not sulk and walk off. Make a scene by throwing a violent tantrum. When people have so obviously upset you despite your best efforts to instruct them in how to behave there is nothing better than to bring them back into line by throwing a monumental wobbler.

I have seen some exceptional executive tantrums, from smashing fists down on desks to boardroom chairs and projection equipment being thrown around meeting rooms. The most wonderful tantrum I have heard of is one thrown by Tom Siebel of the eponymous Siebel Corporation, a giant application software company, who met an ex-executive, Dr Steve Garnett, in the lobby of a San Francisco hotel by chance.

Garnett had recently left Siebel's employ after pocketing a few tens of millions of dollars from stock options and had joined a competitive start-up company. As one of the few likeable successful guys in the business, Garnett had subsequently been followed there by other key Siebel Corp employees. Siebel, who assumed that Garnett was wilfully poaching his staff, was so apoplectic with rage towards him that, as he came down a sweeping staircase to the lobby flanked by his bodyguards, he unleashed a torrent of angst upon him: 'Hey, you know what you get when you moon a gorilla?' Garnett had little clue what Siebel was talking about at first, but he did not have to wait long to hear the answer – Seibel screamed 'You get fucked up the assssssss!'

Explosive grandiose behaviour is a key component of the successful bastard's kitbag, and throwing a major tantrum is a great way to show how serious you are about something. Let rip and enjoy.

#3. Never give up – Being ruthless

Bringing out the warrior in you: Techniques to make you fearless

'Let me not look for allies in life's battlefield but to my own strength. Let me not cave in.'   Rabindranath Tagore

51. Harness your fear. Use fear to your advantage. Most people are frightened of lots of things, and many of these fears are irrational. Phobias, such as fear of heights and open spaces, and common fears such as that of public speaking or raising complaints in public are irrational, yet many people suffer with them. Do not allow yourself to be weak like them. Fear nothing.

The best way to destroy any fears you do have is to force yourself to confront them. Do this whenever the opportunity arises and see it through. Such conditioning will, over a short time, build your defences to the point that nothing will bother you. You will have turned your fear to your advantage – turned fear into an opportunity for greater success.

52. Be powerful. Power is energy divided by time. The higher the energy level, and the shorter the time it is applied, the greater the power produced. Keep your energy levels high. Get a reputation for being a driver, a mover and a shaker. You will live your life at high speed so the apparent power you have will be huge.

They say that knowledge is power. This is because it takes energy to turn information into knowledge. If you can have knowledge instantaneously that would have taken much time to acquire, that knowledge has great power invested in it.

Physical power is useful if you possess it, and at the very least you must appear to be strong to others. Never accept that you have any weaknesses and push yourself forward on your strengths, whatever they are.

53. Lead from the front. Set the right example of leadership and demonstrating what you want by leading from the front. Imagine yourself as a military commander in days of old. Not like one of those hapless First World War generals, sitting in his headquarters quaffing alcohol and toasting muffins on an open fire –get back to Roman times, when Barbarians and the Roman legions alike were led by warriors.

With luck, once you have led from the front once or twice people will get the picture and you can go back to relaxing and enjoying the spoils from the labour of others, but you must first set the standard for others to aspire to. People will follow idiots happily into hazardous conditions – against their better judgement, and even if they know the leader is wrong – if their leader appears confident, vocal and determined. They will do this to avoid a difficult confrontation with the leader and because they do not believe in themselves strongly enough to take a stand.

54. Fear no one. I have never backed down from confrontation and neither should you. In my experience, pain is relative to your belief in your own invincibility. Go in hard and you will not get hurt. I like to remind myself that everyone has to shit, even the important people. It provides an endearingly powerful image when you realise that everyone is built the same way as you.

Everyone is insecure, concerned about their inadequacies and fearful of something more powerful than themselves. Successful bastards just hide it better than others. If you show no signs of weakness and never back-down, the lowliest David can beat the biggest, baddest Goliath.

55. Ignore pain. Pain comes in two different forms – physical pain and mental anguish. We all feel pain and some are better at managing it than others. You need to develop a thick enough skin to ignore pain, whatever form it takes. You are unlikely to get much physical pain, unless your profession is martial or heavily manual, so I will concentrate on pain that is caused by mental anguish.

De-sensitise yourself to the suffering of others, in much the same way that any doctor has to. You also need to apply this same level of attention towards your own ability to deal with the painful challenges. You have to be strong, powerful and forceful and to back up those characteristics with strong defences.

Never allow yourself to be ill. It is bad for business. I know that with the power of positive thinking and a sensible approach to living, your body can handle phenomenal pressures without breaking down. The day you decide that it is all too much, that you just cannot stand it any more, that you worry about what other people think of you, and so on, will be the day your defences come crashing down. Your immune system will collapse and you will become ill. On the other hand, if you ignore pain, stay positive, refuse to give in to illness, you will stay strong and healthy.

Building energy and creating action: Techniques to make you more incisive

'Along with a strong belief in your own inner voice, you also need laser-like focus combined with unwavering determination.'
Larry Flynt

56. Be direct. The biggest mistake anyone can make is to approach a situation in a round-about way. Be concise. When you speak, make only the most salient points as single, stand-alone, direct messages. If you ask a question, make it probing and direct, but open enough to strike fear into whoever has to respond. Never let them off with a simple yes or no answer. Get to the point and leave no ambiguity in what you say.

57. Be precise. If you are direct, you are already halfway to being precise. Make sure that the facts you use are clear, correct and unambiguous. This will mean, naturally, that you will say less and the content of your communication will have a greater impact. When you talk, people will listen. If you do not know the answer or having nothing of substance to add, avoid bullshit, just keep quiet. Precision must become a way of life for you.

58. Be focused. Only focus on those things that hold your interest, where you can add value and that will improve your personal position in life. Make sure you know what these things are. When you are focused you are formidable. People will come to realise that if you really want something, you will achieve it.

Avoid distractions and people who enjoy distraction. Concentrate on completing and finishing things, not leaving them hanging.

him back to school to get it. That in itself is perhaps not surprising, but the trip from home to school, being from Geelong to Sydney, was a 1,200-mile round trip. Kerry telegraphed his father later: 'Arrived Melbourne safely, no love, Kerry.' Delightful.

Take your punishment with grace and dish it out with zeal. It makes for a much richer life experience.

#4. Keep everyone guessing – Being unpredictable

Creating mystery: Techniques to make you more enigmatic

'I have come to believe that the whole world is… a harmless enigma that is made terrible by our own mad attempt to interpret it as though it had an underlying truth.'   Umberto Eco

76. Be complicated. The best way to keep people guessing is to be complicated in your behaviour. Develop hidden depths. Swing your moods and change your preferences. Re-invent yourself every few years and try

Erik's favourite bullying technique was to ask you where you were every time he spoke to you on your mobile telephone. It had a curiously painful impact on you when on the receiving end. It implied that he wanted you to realise that you were not to have any fun whilst working for him. 'Where are you?' would trigger deep anxiety in the receiver, and make that person squirm to explain how busy they were working for him.

When you become self-made you will need to operate like Erik. People need to be worried about what you are capable of and that you will not hesitate to hurt them in some way if you do not perform to their fullest satisfaction. You need to have left a lot of people in your wake.

75. Punish severely. Most people appreciate that punishment is good for them. They expect it and benefit from it. I had the pleasure of surviving a Catholic school run by the De La Salle Brotherhood, which seemed to me to be a club where deviant sadists and pederasts go to act out their fantasies on children.

Corporal punishment was good for me. It built my resilience to pain and sharpened my competitive skills. For many years, I topped the league table of schoolboys who had been struck by teachers most often. I even racked up a maximum score in more than one school week by receiving the maximum punishment – 'getting six' as it was known – each and every day.

I love the story of Sir Kerry Packer, the late Australian billionaire media mogul and son of Sir Frank Packer, who once forgot his tennis racket on coming home from boarding school for his holiday. Sir Frank, being a man to instil serious discipline in his sons, immediately sent

I want you to die happy in the knowledge that you gave everything you did, everything you had. Imagine the satisfaction that this will bring. A life lived well, to the full, complete and full of real achievement.

63. Be driven. In my experience, whenever somebody is in your circle and combines hard work with an intelligent application and overcomes all obstacles along the way, they are described as driven. You need to be driven to succeed – obviously, clearly and continuously. If people call you driven, you will have achieved your aim.

64. Be committed. Here is a dilemma. You want to be committed and work hard to achieve your aims, but be lazy and have loads of leisure time at the same time.

This might seem like an insoluble conundrum, but it is not. Simply be committed to things that other people deliver for you.

Leverage your opportunities by setting the framework of action and objectives and then get the others to deliver. You may have to work intensively for short periods at the beginning, but the bulk of the work will be delivered by others, so this should not be too painful for you. As Franklin D Roosevelt once said: 'When you come to the end of your rope, tie a knot and hang on.'

65. Be disciplined. I have found that discipline is one of the critical ingredients in life, but one that is malleable. One person's discipline is another's disorganisation. You will need to discipline yourself to your own standards. The trick that will change your life is to make sure that you do things every day. The cumulative effect of daily practice is dramatic and stunning. I practice martial arts and meditation daily, not intensively, but I do it every day. The power that this builds within me is quite awesome and allows me to perform what would appear impossible feats of strength and destruction.

There is an energy inside you that will be unleashed with daily practice of whatever you do. If you write well, do it daily; if you sing well do it daily; if you pick good stocks or horses, do it daily. You will, I guarantee, be amazed at the ways in which your skills improve with daily practice, even with minimal efforts.

Do yourself the favour of your lifetime and be more disciplined, doing what you enjoy and do best, every day.

Creating a blame culture: Techniques to make you more unforgiving

'It is a purely relative matter where one draws the plimsoll-line of condemnation, and if you find the whole of humanity falls below it you have simply made a mistake and drawn it too high. And are probably below it yourself.' **Frances Partridge**

66. Blame everyone but yourself. Look for scapegoats at the first sign of failure. Look for people who can be blamed. These people are everywhere. They will usually be the ones that look up to you, are obedient and faithful, and have their noses wedged firmly up your backside – the 'Yes Men.' The beauty of blaming 'Yes Men' is that when you ask them if it was their fault, they will usually say 'Yes' just to please you.

Do not waste time criticising people's behaviour, performance or work. It is them whom you should criticise, not their actions or results. The world is full of wannabes – no-hopers who fail to take responsibility for their own behaviour, performance or quality of work. Do not bother to waste your time wrapping things in cotton wool when criticising someone.

In a job I had many years ago, my team were responsible for developing and implementing a complex computer system for a major UK bank. The IT director was one hell of a successful bastard when it came to managing suppliers. Nothing was ever good enough, and we had to bend over backwards to just keep this guy off our case.

Every one of our monthly review meetings would open with this guy saying: 'I was disappointed...' And he would then follow up with negative criticism of all and sundry. It was so awful that to amuse ourselves we used to count the number of times he would say the word 'disappointed' and measure our success on that value, relative to the value gained at the last meeting. After a few such meetings we decided to turn the tables, and me and the guy managing the project came up with the aim of saying the word first, before he could, and then saying it more times than he did during the meeting itself.

We would open the meeting by saying how disappointed we were that his personal assistant was unwell and how disappointed we were that the coffee machine appeared to be out of order, or that the train was late, or the lift took ages to arrive. It was all we could do to keep ourselves from breaking down in hysterics when his usual reply was something like 'Forget about being disappointed about the coffee machine, I am disappointed that you failed to deliver the last software release on Tuesday evening as planned…' It did not have much impact on the meeting, or his volume of criticism, but it was great fun and that is more important, especially during tough times.

For study purposes watch any American manager carry out a performance appraisal of one his or her staff or any successful bastard that is employing you on a contract to do work that his or her people are incapable of doing themselves.

66. Never allow an appeal. There is never any need for the people who you have blamed to apologise. No excuses are necessary – none will be accepted. Put a sign up on the wall of your office to make sure everyone realises this. Your decision is final. The buck stops with you, there is no room for any appeal, so do not entertain one.

Learn to block out the word 'sorry' should anyone be foolish enough to use it. Of course they are bloody sorry, and so they should be. They should have thought about that before they did whatever they did.

For study purposes simply watch any judge in a region of the world that orders the death penalty for drug traffickers.

68. Write people off. No excuses or apologies should ever be accepted, no appeals entertained, and not just now – forever. Dismiss the people from your life that fail you and move on. You should not worry about this. There will be many other people, better people, who will want to share in your success and try even harder than the last to please you, so waste no time in writing people off permanently if they fail.

For study purposes, watch a head teacher

What if everyone in a firm knew exactly what everyone else earned? What if the designs of everything ever made were common knowledge – how would one product ever be differentiated from another? Why would anyone invest in building anything new and revolutionary, if the intellectual property was immediately shared with everyone?

We all need secrecy at every level of our lives. Find me two people who live together who have never held a secret from one another, and I will be surprised.

As a successful bastard, secrecy is your weapon. You do not want anyone knowing what you think, what you are planning or how you intend to behave in the future.

Be like the Barclay brothers, Sir David and Sir Frederick – the secretive, some might say reclusive, businessmen who own the Ritz Hotel in London, several newspapers and magazines, including *The Daily Telegraph* and *The Spectator* and their flagship retail empire, Littlewoods. The painters and decorators turned mega-businessmen are famous for avoiding publicity and rarely give interviews. They live on their own island, Brecqhou – one of the Channel Islands – which is west of Sark. In 2007, their estimated wealth was £1.8 billion. They operate through complex offshore companies, financial trusts and investment vehicles.

78. Be eccentric. I would not advise you getting quite as eccentric as say, David Icke. I would not recommend believing and then writing that there are a race of reptilian humanoids known as the Babylonian Brotherhood that lead world events and that many prominent figures are reptilian, not to do the same thing too often. The most colourful and interesting people you know will have varied tastes and a style that is difficult to imitate. You never quite know what they will do next. They are unpredictable and enjoy variety.

Develop multiple, and what might appear conflicting, interests and hobbies. Invest time and money in many different projects. Diversify your exposure to people from all walks of life and levels of society. Gain pleasure from many things and have an eclectic taste for music and reading. Get the tabloids and the broadsheets, read 'get rich quick' books and Karl Marx.

Keep moving, changing and re-directing what you do. At the very least you will confuse the opposition; at best you will be able to take any stance honourably when it suits you.

77. Be secretive. Secrecy is a requirement for humankind to survive. Certain types of information must be kept secret to keep society in order and people comfortably in their place. All governments keep secrets, all employers keep secrets and all individuals keep secrets.

Imagine a government that had no secrets. What would an opposing political party or terrorist group do with it? Clearly, they would use it against their 'enemy' to further their own aims. We would not want Osama Bin Laden knowing the locations and launch codes for our nuclear weapons arsenal. If it was well known how to get into the vaults of the Central Bank, the nation's money would not be safe there.

If the long-term strategies for major companies were well known, where would their competitive edge be derived from?

73. Spread vicious rumours. I have usually found that rumours I have heard turn out to be true. As my dear late grandmother, Hilda, used to say 'there's no smoke without fire.' She applied this to anyone and everyone that she suspected was responsible for anything she disapproved of, which was just about everything. In reality, most people feel this way. If there is a hint of something untoward about someone, then the chances are it is probably true.

Being a successful bastard is all about seizing opportunity and winning against the competition that will inevitably pursue you. You want to beat all others to the prize. If you choose to unfairly undermine your opponents in the process, all the better – and there is no better way to undermine people than to spread vicious rumours about them.

It is effortless to start or simply pass on a

vicious rumour about someone. The grapevine and gossip network will do the rest for you. You can just sit back and wait. Pick a subject that is very difficult to prove or disprove to taint your opponents with. If it is difficult or near impossible to prove or disprove it, it can be as distasteful and unbelievable as you like.

Cast aspersions about the mental health or sexual orientation of your opponent or make up a story about his or her penchant for illegal narcotics. No one will ever question you for hard evidence, if they do, say simply that someone close to them told you.

I have been aware of people being accused of everything from early-morning drinking, fiddling expenses, having their had genitals pierced and skiving on the golf course to extremes such as suffering from hard-drug addiction, being active in the 'swinging' scene, having paedophiliac tendencies and even practicing bestiality with their pets. On every occasion I have assumed these vile rumours to be untrue, yet a part of me has said, 'Hmmm, maybe, just maybe…'

It is human nature to believe the worst about people, and nothing makes for a more exciting conversation than one laced with salacious gossip.

For study purposes, watch any group of people who meet regularly on the occasion that one person does not show up, or simply stand in a corridor, a rest-room or a smoking area and just keep your ears pricked.

74. Bully the weak. One nice thing about being all-powerful and super-successful is that, by definition, everyone else is weak by comparison. Bullying the weak is just the same as bullying anyone around you.

If you want to get on in life, you have to be prepared to bully people. You can call this 'using your powers of persuasion,' 'leadership,' 'direction,' whatever. Make it sound as palatable as you like, but you will need to be a bully to get what you want done. If people find your bullying offensive, that's fine, they are supposed to. Treat them mean, to keep them keen. The weakest people around you will wilt under the pressure. Whether they were on your side or not, it does not matter because both groups deserve your wrath. Weak people need to be bullied out of your way.

I worked with a delightful guy called Erik Tiller, a successful Norwegian venture capitalist who had some fantastic ways to bully people. The fact that he was stocky to the point of being as wide as he was tall, helped to give him that menacing edge.

Erik's favourite bullying technique was to ask you where you were every time he spoke to you on your mobile telephone. It had a curiously painful impact on you when on the receiving end. It implied that he wanted you to realise that you were not to have any fun whilst working for him. 'Where are you?' would trigger deep anxiety in the receiver, and make that person squirm to explain how busy they were working for him.

When you become self-made you will need to operate like Erik. People need to be worried about what you are capable of and that you will not hesitate to hurt them in some way if you do not perform to their fullest satisfaction. You need to have left a lot of people in your wake.

75. Punish severely. Most people appreciate that punishment is good for them. They expect it and benefit from it. I had the pleasure of surviving a Catholic school run by the De La Salle Brotherhood, which seemed to me to be a club where deviant sadists and pederasts go to act out their fantasies on children.

Corporal punishment was good for me. It built my resilience to pain and sharpened my competitive skills. For many years, I topped the league table of schoolboys who had been struck by teachers most often. I even racked up a maximum score in more than one school week by receiving the maximum punishment – 'getting six' as it was known – each and every day.

I love the story of Sir Kerry Packer, the late Australian billionaire media mogul and son of Sir Frank Packer, who once forgot his tennis racket on coming home from boarding school for his holiday. Sir Frank, being a man to instil serious discipline in his sons, immediately sent him back to school to get it. That in itself is perhaps not surprising, but the trip from home to school, being from Geelong to Sydney, was a 1,200-mile round trip. Kerry telegraphed his father later: 'Arrived Melbourne safely, no love, Kerry.' Delightful.

Take your punishment with grace and dish it out with zeal. It makes for a much richer life experience.

#4. Keep everyone guessing – Being unpredictable

Creating mystery: Techniques to make you more enigmatic

'I have come to believe that the whole world is… a harmless enigma that is made terrible by our own mad attempt to interpret it as though it had an underlying truth.' **Umberto Eco**

76. Be complicated. The best way to keep people guessing is to be complicated in your behaviour. Develop hidden depths. Swing your moods and change your preferences. Re-invent yourself every few years and try not to do the same thing too often. The most colourful and interesting people you know will have varied tastes and a style that is difficult to imitate. You never quite know what they will do next. They are unpredictable and enjoy variety.

Develop multiple, and what might appear conflicting, interests and hobbies. Invest time and money in many different projects. Diversify your exposure to people from all walks of life and levels of society. Gain pleasure from many things and have an eclectic taste for music and reading. Get the tabloids and the broadsheets, read 'get rich quick' books and Karl Marx.

Keep moving, changing and re-directing what you do. At the very least you will confuse the opposition; at best you will be able to take any stance honourably when it suits you.

77. Be secretive. Secrecy is a requirement for humankind to survive. Certain types of information must be kept secret to keep society in order and people comfortably in their place. All governments keep secrets, all employers keep secrets and all individuals keep secrets.

Imagine a government that had no secrets. What would an opposing political party or terrorist group do with it? Clearly, they would use it against their 'enemy' to further their own aims. We would not want Osama Bin Laden knowing the locations and launch codes for our nuclear weapons arsenal. If it was well known how to get into the vaults of the Central Bank, the nation's money would not be safe there.

If the long-term strategies for major companies were well known, where would their competitive edge be derived from?

What if everyone in a firm knew exactly what everyone else earned? What if the designs of everything ever made were common knowledge – how would one product ever be differentiated from another? Why would anyone invest in building anything new and revolutionary, if the intellectual property was immediately shared with everyone?

We all need secrecy at every level of our lives. Find me two people who live together who have never held a secret from one another, and I will be surprised.

As a successful bastard, secrecy is your weapon. You do not want anyone knowing what you think, what you are planning or how you intend to behave in the future.

Be like the Barclay brothers, Sir David and Sir Frederick – the secretive, some might say reclusive, businessmen who own the Ritz Hotel in London, several newspapers and magazines, including *The Daily Telegraph* and *The Spectator* and their flagship retail empire, Littlewoods. The painters and decorators turned mega-businessmen are famous for avoiding publicity and rarely give interviews. They live on their own island, Brecqhou – one of the Channel Islands – which is west of Sark. In 2007, their estimated wealth was £1.8 billion. They operate through complex offshore companies, financial trusts and investment vehicles.

78. Be eccentric. I would not advise you getting quite as eccentric as say, David Icke. I would not recommend believing and then writing that there are a race of reptilian humanoids known as the Babylonian Brotherhood that lead world events and that many prominent figures are reptilian, including George W Bush, HRH Queen Elizabeth II, Kris Kristofferson and Boxcar Willie. Bless him, but David Icke is clearly mentally ill.

You need to be eccentric in the manner of old judges, very wealthy business people and landed gentry. Develop a passion for things that are a little bizarre. Collect weird objects, follow obscure sports and maintain a belief that makes people's hair curl. Insist on wearing a particular item of clothing that stands out unusually, regardless of the occasion. Be a little bit Howard Hughes.

For study purposes, watch anyone with a triple-barrelled surname or who insists people use their middle initial when introducing them to others.

79. Embrace change. Change is part of daily life in the modern world. Adapting to what is happening around you is essential to your survival. Without it you cannot prosper.

The greatest fortunes have been made by people who have exploited major changes in the world. Mining, oil, steel, railroads, cotton, tobacco, tea, cars, newspapers, plastics, drugs, media, telecommunications, technology, biotechnology and most recently the Internet have all been the root of personal fortune for many. Jump on the new industries and exploit them before others do.

If you have any clue about what is coming next, invest money and time in it. Those people who spotted the Internet early and were lucky enough to invest in the search engine Google at flotation in August 2004, for example, will have seen a US$100 investment grow to more than US$600 today. If you had invested the same amount in the telecommunications giant Cisco

Systems in 1990, it would be worth more than US$53,000 in 2007 and all without you having lifted a finger.

80. Be independent. If you follow the crowd you will simply end up an indistinguishable part of it. You want to be different. You want to be part of that exclusive club of successful bastards. You may think this group is a crowd but they are a group of individuals and not a crowd. They will have made individual fortunes in unique ways and operate lives that are unlike those lived as one of the masses.

Be a trend-setter, have your own views and maintain an independence from those around you. Use your independence as a beacon to show your uniqueness.

Using your cloak and dagger: Techniques to make you more deceptive

'A little inaccuracy sometimes saves a lot of explanation.'   H H Munro

81. Manipulate people. Change your style to meet the needs of a situation. Manipulate people to your way of thinking by adapting yourself to fit in with what they want to see.

Watch Gordon Brown, or any politician for that matter, as they travel around the country, and see how they change the way they speak depending on the region that is being visited or the group that is being addressed. Watch any state-appointed defence barrister when talking to someone with no qualifications, no family and no job.

82. Be two-faced. Being duplicitous or two-faced is a necessary evil. As a CEO you have responsibilities to the shareholders and the employees. You cannot treat both groups of people the same way. You have to have more than one face.

If you have children, the old saying 'Do as I say, not as I do' applies. You would not be happy letting your seven-year-old child smoke, even if you do yourself. We all have to have multiple faces, not just two.

Since we know everyone is two-faced or worse, why not exploit that to your advantage. Put the face on that suits the person you are with.

For study purposes, listen to a Glaswegian talking to a fellow Glaswegian. Then listen to them talking to an Englishman. One will be an unintelligible monologue of grunts and the other a rhythmical rendition like that of an 'old-school' English TV newsreader.

83. Confuse people. The fundamental art of deception is based on confusing people. You need to move them to a place where they are unable to anticipate what is going to happen next. You need to wrong-foot people and keep them off balance in the same way that a professional football player can wrong-foot a defender simply by looking one way and going another.

84. Be charming. What is it that makes us think someone is charming? I believe it is one thing above all that makes someone appear charming. They genuinely listen to you. What better way to charm someone than let them talk about themselves and appear to be genuinely interested in what they say. The challenge for you is to work out who to be charming with and whom you need not bother with. I recommend you be charming to anyone you live with, your mother and anyone you are selling something to. You can be as nasty as you like to everyone else.

For study purposes watch anyone who is trying to get you into bed or sell you something that you do not need. Maybe you can do both at the same time?

85. Cheat at everything. Even Carl Lewis, the vocal anti-doping, multiple-gold medallist sprinter, took performance-enhancing drugs. He cheated, was found out and got away with it. Over-the-counter herbal cold medicine was to blame apparently. The positive results occurred at the Olympic Trials in July 1988 where athletes were required to declare on the drug-testing forms 'over-the-counter medication, prescription drugs and any other substances you have taken by mouth, injection or by suppository,' which Mr Lewis failed to do.

It was revealed that Lewis tested positive

three times before the 1988 Olympics in Seoul, Korea – for pseudoephedrine, ephedrine and phenylpropanolamine – all of which were banned stimulants. Lewis was then banned from the 1988 Olympics and from any other competition for six months. Subsequently, the US Olympic Committee accepted his claim of inadvertent use and overturned the decision.

I think it all the more amusing that in the 100 metres final at the Seoul Olympics, Ben Johnson, the Canadian sprinter, won Gold and set a new World Record. However, Johnson was subsequently stripped of his World Record and of his gold medal, both of which were handed to second place Lewis instead, when Johnson tested positive for performance-enhancing drugs. Johnson's records have been erased from history, while Lewis's remain.

Letting people down: Techniques to make you less reliable

'Figures do not lie, but liars figure.'
Oscar Wilde

86. Be insincere. If you can fake sincerity, you can fake anything. Master this skill. For study purposes, watch HRH Queen Elizabeth when meeting a member of the public or a politician talking to a member of the great unwashed – the unemployed.

87. Be imprecise. Follow the example set by all the world's politicians. Develop the ability to avoid answering questions, but still provide animated and compelling responses. The trick is to always know what you want to say and say that. If you do not like the question, simply prefix what you would like to say with phrases like:

'It's more a case of...'

'You have missed the most important point, which is…'

'The problem has less to do with <reference the question> than it has to do with…'

If all else fails: 'I am not at liberty to comment at this time' works wonders.

For study purposes, watch any sub-committee of any Government, anywhere, investigating an important suspected breach of public trust.

88. Fail to keep promises. Do not worry about quality, delivering on time, delivering to specification or meeting commitments. Get other people to worry about that stuff for you. For study purposes read any political party's manifesto and compare it to what is delivered after a few years in office.

89. Tell big lies. Tell lies a lot. Tell a lot of

lies. Do you know anyone who has never told a lie? No – neither do I. We all lie. Just watch the film *Liar, Liar* starring Jim Carrey. The nice thing about lying is that most people believe you. It is human nature. Little white lies, all the time. A story embellished, a detail changed, an honest opinion not expressed to avoid upsetting a loved one.

We are programmed to lie and we are pretty damned good at it. The little lies are OK, big lies are great. When people believe them it can have a major impact in your favour.

I have worked with many professionals who lie routinely and still hold their jobs down. Advisors who lie about their knowledge, lawyers who lie about what they know, managers who lie about what is going to happen to their employees, company owners who lie about their plans and results, Presidents and Prime Ministers who lie about matters of state, senior policemen who lie under oath. I am sure you do as well.

Self-preservation and the desire to improve our own position force us to lie. There is no need to feel ashamed about telling big lies. On the contrary, you should exploit the opportunity and just do what all successful bastards do, and do it better than them.

For study purposes watch anyone in an important and trusted position who is under threat and wait for their lips to move.

90. Live a lie. People will be fascinated to discover that you are an international canoe instructor, black-belted martial artist in more than one style, an accomplished musician, a painter, a one-time Junior Wimbledon champion and Falklands war veteran.

Maybe you think that is a hard list of accomplishments to pretend you have. A professional colleague of mine, who was 32 years old in 1992, claimed all this at that time and got away with it. The more complex and confusing the falsehoods you create about yourself, the less likely anyone will be able to fathom fact from fiction.

For study practice, read any unauthorised biography of anyone in the public eye.

Cooking the books: Techniques to make you more dishonest
'Behind every great fortune there is a crime.' **Honore de Balzac**

91. Evade tax. Only two things in life are certain: death and taxes. Not true. Death maybe – taxes most definitely not. Almost every country's taxation system looks favourably on those who purport to create wealth for others. Some look so favourably on the wealthy that they become tax-havens for the obscenely rich and powerful: Monaco, the Channel Islands, the Cayman Islands, Bermuda, etc…

According to research published by the Tax Justice Network in 2005, the estimated wealth 'openly' held in tax havens is costing governments around the world up to US$255 billion annually in lost tax revenues. This does not include corporate tax 'hidden' there, so the number is substantially higher in reality.

US$255 billion could provide adequate health services for every person in the world every year or permanently eradicate world poverty within six years. It is quite simply a staggering amount of money.

You should not therefore worry about evading tax yourself. Your impact on the world will be small in comparison and the benefits to you will be great.

Whether you stay in your native country, or become a tax exile, when you have a lot of money you will pay less tax than the average person. In the UK, for instance, if you can afford to leave money in your company for four years you only pay 10% tax, instead of the usual 40-50%.

Imagine that you earn £1m a year, which many successful bastards do. That means you will be several thousand pounds *per week* better off for burying your money in your company and then extracting it just a few years later. Forget Pay As You Earn, go self-employed and start your own company.

I remember reading about that successful bastard Mohammed Al Fayed, owner of Harrods, the Paris Ritz and Fulham Football Club to name just three of his flagship enterprises. Until recently, Al Fayed had an 'agreement' with the Inland Revenue as a resident in the UK that he would pay £250,000 income tax each year and they would not investigate his earnings further. That means that he was assessed as if he was earning around the equivalent of £650,000 annually if paying at 40% or at worst £2.5 million if paying at 10%. With what this guy owns and the lifestyle he supports he just has to be earning 100 times that, but because of his 'arrangement' he is evading tax within the law.

Make an arrangement with the tax authorities if you like the country in which your are living. They know that if they do not agree, you will simply hide it all from them anyway in some labyrinth of holding companies and offshore financial trusts. Or, just move somewhere else that is more kind towards you.

If you have to relocate, I recommend moving to Monaco, where income tax is a pleasing 0%, but you can only get in if you can show a £1 million or so in the bank beforehand, so get busy earning it now.

92. Be corrupt. You may not be lucky enough to be a Head of State and relieve your country of a chunk of its national wealth like many successful bastards, but you do not have to be at the top of things to benefit. So much is available to people who are corrupt.

In 1999 F Hoffmann-La Roche Ltd, currently the sixth largest pharmaceutical company in the world, pleaded guilty and agreed to pay a record US$500 million fine and BASF pleaded guilty and agreed to pay a $225 million fine, for leading a worldwide conspiracy to fix, raise and maintain prices, rig bids for contracts and allocate market shares for vitamin products. If you are lucky enough to lead a major corporation, the opportunities to act in a corrupt manner are endless. Anyone in power will wish to feather their own nests.

93. Cook the books. There are so many cases of companies cooking the books and individuals at the top of the company benefiting from the fraud that hundreds of books have been written about them. And these are just the cases we know about. Here are three of the best, in summary.

In 1996, Daiwa Bank pleaded guilty to multiple felonies and paid a US$340 million criminal fine – the largest ever at that time – for covering up massive securities trading losses on two separate occasions and deceiving and defrauding bank regulators.

In December 2001, the energy giant Enron

filed for then the biggest bankruptcy in US history. Enron's collapse resulted in 20,000 employees losing their jobs. Many of those also lost their life savings, having been encouraged by their CEO, Kenneth Lay, to buy stock at a time he was dumping his. Investors worldwide also lost billions.

Lay, who earned US$42.4 million in 1999 and had sold more than US$300 million of Enron stock options since 1989, was brought to trial and found guilty on 10 counts of criminal conspiracy, fraud and for making false financial statements. Sentencing was scheduled to take in October 2006, and he faced up to 20 years in prison for his crimes. However, he died of a heart attack at his home in Aspen, Colorado, on July 5, 2006, before the sentence was given. Lay subsequently had his conviction 'vacated' which, despite many protests, means that his record is not formally blemished.

On July 21, 2002, WorldCom – one of the largest telecommunications in the world – filed for Chapter 11 bankruptcy protection, at the time the largest such filing in US history. WorldCom's audit department had uncovered a US$3.8 billion fraud in June 2002, during a routine examination of company accounts. This later turned out to be more like US$11 billion.

From 1999 through May 2002, under the direction of Bernie Ebbers (CEO), Scott Sullivan (CFO), David Myers (Controller) and Buford Yates (Director of General Accounting), the company had used fraudulent accounting methods to make its declining financial condition look instead like growth and increasing profitability by under-reporting costs and failing to expense them properly. Their auditors were the now defunct and discredited Arthur Andersen, who had been dissolved following the collapse of Enron.

Bernie Ebbers made some spectacular personal gains from WorldCom before he was found out and brought to justice. At his peak in early 1999, Ebbers was worth an estimated US$1.4 billion. His personal holdings included ownership of Canada's biggest ranch, which was bigger than Wales; several farms, timber forests and lumber companies; a yacht builder; nine hotels; a trucking company; and a hockey team. All of these businesses were funded by his WorldCom stock. As WorldCom stock plummeted during 2001, Bernie Ebbers persuaded the board of directors to provide him corporate loans and guarantees of more than US$400 million to cover problems he had servicing this debt.

However, Bernie got bashed up badly for being a naughty boy. On September 6, 2006, he was sentenced to 25-years in prison. He now languishes in low-security incarceration at Oakdale Federal Correctional Institution in Oakdale, Louisiana, having driven himself there in his Mercedes. The earliest date he will be considered for parole is 2028 when he will be 85 years old.

If all you know is how to be a cowboy, do not let that affect your confidence when applying to be a global corporate leader. Just make sure you don't spend all your time on the ranch.

94. Steal everything. Most people do not have original thoughts and are not creative. Most people are too swept up in the daily shit-storm of life to lift their heads out and think of something new. Most new ideas are adapted from old ones. Changed a little maybe, but stolen all the same.

Most people assume that Hoover invented the vacuum cleaner, but it was a chap called Hubert Cecil Booth who invented the machine in 1900. Like so many inventions, it was copied and adapted from someone else's idea. Booth had watched a demonstration on a train at St Pancras station of a device aimed at replacing the dustpan and broom. This device blew dust into a container. It sparked an idea in Booth's head – why not suck it up, rather than blow it around? Booth went home and placed a damp cloth over the arm of his chair and using his mouth and lungs literally sucked through the cloth. On seeing the results, his idea for the vacuum cleaner was born. Within one year, Booth had built and patented his first vacuum cleaner, which he called the Puffing Billy – a massive machine that had to be carried on a horse-drawn cart.

95. Spy on everyone. If you are not able

to know something that no one else knows, simply know something that no one else knows you know by spying on them.

There have been many cases publicised about spying, mainly where one government spies on another. There are multiple government agencies openly accountable for organising spying. It is no surprise that spying is an every day fact of life.

It has been reported that the UK's Government Communications Headquarters (GCHQ) 'listens in' to every telephone conversation and reads every e-mail sent or received in the UK and automatically assesses them for potential threats and criminal activity.

Ask any drug dealer or career criminal how many phones they use and how often they change them if you do not believe me.

Taking and sharing risks: Techniques to make you more dangerous

'Playing safe is only playing.'   **Chuck Olson**

96. Taking big risks. If you do not like risk, do not bother getting up in the morning. Stay in bed, you will be safe there. If you decide to get up and go out, then embrace risk at every turn. The trick is not to be risk averse, but be risk aware.

Develop risk mitigation strategies for each venture that presents itself. Always have a contingency plan, be prepared for things to go wrong and know what to say and do before the bad things happen. Once you are comfortable with taking risks, take even bigger ones. Push the envelope on it. Big risk, well managed, delivers big returns.

97. Live life on the edge. Stress is good for you. Stress is a normal experience. The word 'stress' was first coined in relation to human beings in 1935, before that it was only ever used by engineers.

Be a fatalist – you are going to die for sure sometime. Better to live a day as lion than a lifetime as a sheep. You are here for a good time, not for a long time. Your life will pass you by in an instant; do not waste time worrying about the consequences of your actions. Just get on with it.

There are so many scaremongering warnings about everything, including every food you can think of – meat, sugar, butter, eggs and fats; most things pleasurable, including alcohol, smoking, narcotics, rock music and sex; most things in everyday use, including microwave ovens, aerosol cans, computer screens, mobile phones and motor cars; and for every possible lifestyle, including inactivity, jogging, working hard and playing sports… The list is truly endless.

Ignore it all. Worrying about it will add an unnecessary burden to your life. If you smoke, then smoke. If you enjoy over-eating, indulge. Death has its eye on you regardless and with all the possible ways to die, who knows which one it will be.

When you are wealthy and powerful you can survive things that would kill ordinary people thanks to the investment you will make in keeping yourself alive using artificial means. Use your wealth to provide yourself that extra chance over the masses. Detoxify yourself a few times every year with a total blood transfusion, or like Rod Stewart, have regular MRI scans to detect even the minutest change in the health of your vital organs. Get yourself a fully staffed medical team at home like Hugh Hefner, of Playboy fame. You can afford to live life right on the edge and you deserve the opportunity.

98. Move at high speed. It is not the big that eats the small. It is the fast that eats the slow. Get yourself, your idea, your product or your company moving fastest in its market. Focus on the opportunity, make the decision and then execute swiftly. If you do things quickly, you will have first mover advantages. You will be able to cream off the best return from taking the higher risk.

99. Abuse your power. Power corrupts and absolute power corrupts absolutely as we know. When you are powerful, you will not be able to help yourself. You will abuse your power. It may start at first with some practical jokes to amuse yourself and move onto full scale abuse of those around you.

What is the point of having power if with it come no advantages? The two things are inseparably linked. In fact, the definition of power itself includes a built-in authority to abuse and exploit others. Do not be shy about this; just get on with enjoying it.

100. Endanger others. You are important to yourself and to those around you. So, if you have the option, endanger others before endangering yourself.

Take enormous risks, ideally with other people's money and energy because yours is more precious than theirs. Create a culture where people will follow you over the cliff, or ideally jump off without you, if you say so. It will make their lives more exciting and fulfilling and ironically they will be grateful for it, or at the least reluctantly accept that it was their fault for agreeing to it.

Work the people around you mercilessly hard and expect the impossible from them in terms of work rate and output. Make it clear that their health is not your concern. The most important thing is to get the job done. Disregard safety rules when it suits you, and the job needs to be done by the crazy deadline you have set.

When is the last time you heard of a 'four-star' general being killed in action? Never, right? Does that tell you anything? If not, go back to the beginning and read this book again. Get real.

Successful bastards' website
www.successful-bastards.com

This is the official successful bastards' website, where you can find extra tips, communicate with other like-minded people and tell me about your own experiences of living in the world of successful bastards.

Successful Bastard's Bingo
Learn how successful bastards' behaviour works by playing this game. Pick the biggest bastard you know, watch them and mark off the 'numbers' Bingo-style when they exhibit the trait marked. Try starting with your boss.

Bastardometer
Use this questionnaire to identify how frequently a person displays the habits of successful bastards. Have fun measuring yourself and others and get a formal certificate from the *Society of Successful Bastards*.

INDEX